Hal·Leonard INSTRUMENTAL PLAY-ALONG

AUDIO ACCESS INCLUDED

PLAYBACK+
Speed · Pitch · Balance · Loop

TRUMPET

CLASSIC ROCK

T0087137

Audio Arrangements by Peter Deneff

To access audio visit:
www.halleonard.com/mylibrary

Enter Code
2951-7136-7281-8760

ISBN 978-1-5400-5328-2

HAL·LEONARD®

Visit Hal Leonard Online at
www.halleonard.com

Contact us:
Hal Leonard
7777 West Bluemound Road
Milwaukee, WI 53213
Email: info@halleonard.com

In Europe, contact:
Hal Leonard Europe Limited
42 Wigmore Street
Marylebone, London, W1U 2RN
Email: info@halleonardeurope.com

In Australia, contact:
Hal Leonard Australia Pty. Ltd.
4 Lentara Court
Cheltenham, Victoria, 3192 Australia
Email: info@halleonard.com.au

DON'T FEAR THE REAPER

TRUMPET

Words and Music by
DONALD ROESER

3

FORTUNATE SON

TRUMPET

Words and Music by
JOHN FOGERTY

FREE FALLIN'

TRUMPET

Words and Music by TOM PETTY
and JEFF LYNNE

GO YOUR OWN WAY

TRUMPET

Words and Music by
LINDSEY BUCKINGHAM

IT'S ONLY ROCK AND ROLL
(But I Like It)

TRUMPET

Words and Music by MICK JAGGER
and KEITH RICHARDS

JACK AND DIANE

TRUMPET

Words and Music by
JOHN MELLENCAMP

LAYLA

TRUMPET

Words and Music by ERIC CLAPTON
and JIM GORDON

THE LOGICAL SONG

TRUMPET

Words and Music by RICK DAVIES
and ROGER HODGSON

MONEY

TRUMPET

Words and Music by
ROGER WATERS

MORE THAN A FEELING

TRUMPET

Words and Music by
TOM SCHOLZ

OLD TIME ROCK & ROLL

TRUMPET

Words and Music by GEORGE JACKSON
and THOMAS E. JONES III

MY LIFE

TRUMPET

Words and Music by
BILLY JOEL

RENEGADE

TRUMPET

Words and Music by
TOMMY SHAW

SWEET HOME ALABAMA

TRUMPET

Words and Music by RONNIE VAN ZANT,
ED KING and GARY ROSSINGTON

25 OR 6 TO 4

TRUMPET

Words and Music by
ROBERT LAMM

Your favorite songs are arranged just for solo instrumentalists with this outstanding series. Each book includes great full-accompaniment play-along audio so you can sound just like a pro! Check out www.halleonard.com to see all the titles available.

The Beatles

All You Need Is Love • Blackbird • Day Tripper • Eleanor Rigby • Get Back • Here, There and Everywhere • Hey Jude • I Will • Let It Be • Lucy in the Sky with Diamonds • Ob-La-Di, Ob-La-Da • Penny Lane • Something • Ticket to Ride • Yesterday.

____	00225330	Flute	$14.99
____	00225331	Clarinet	$14.99
____	00225332	Alto Sax	$14.99
____	00225333	Tenor Sax	$14.99
____	00225334	Trumpet	$14.99
____	00225335	Horn	$14.99
____	00225336	Trombone	$14.99
____	00225337	Violin	$14.99
____	00225338	Viola	$14.99
____	00225339	Cello	$14.99

Chart Hits

All About That Bass • All of Me • Happy • Radioactive • Roar • Say Something • Shake It Off • A Sky Full of Stars • Someone like You • Stay with Me • Thinking Out Loud • Uptown Funk.

____	00146207	Flute	$12.99
____	00146208	Clarinet	$12.99
____	00146209	Alto Sax	$12.99
____	00146210	Tenor Sax	$12.99
____	00146211	Trumpet	$12.99
____	00146212	Horn	$12.99
____	00146213	Trombone	$12.99
____	00146214	Violin	$12.99
____	00146215	Viola	$12.99
____	00146216	Cello	$12.99

Disney Greats

Arabian Nights • Hawaiian Roller Coaster Ride • It's a Small World • Look Through My Eyes • Yo Ho (A Pirate's Life for Me) • and more.

____	00841934	Flute	$12.99
____	00841935	Clarinet	$12.99
____	00841936	Alto Sax	$12.99
____	00841937	Tenor Sax	$12.95
____	00841938	Trumpet	$12.99
____	00841939	Horn	$12.99
____	00841940	Trombone	$12.99
____	00841941	Violin	$12.99
____	00841942	Viola	$12.99
____	00841943	Cello	$12.99
____	00842078	Oboe	$12.99

The Greatest Showman

Come Alive • From Now On • The Greatest Show • A Million Dreams • Never Enough • The Other Side • Rewrite the Stars • This Is Me • Tightrope.

____	00277389	Flute	$14.99
____	00277390	Clarinet	$14.99
____	00277391	Alto Sax	$14.99
____	00277392	Tenor Sax	$14.99
____	00277393	Trumpet	$14.99
____	00277394	Horn	$14.99
____	00277395	Trombone	$14.99
____	00277396	Violin	$14.99
____	00277397	Viola	$14.99
____	00277398	Cello	$14.99

Movie and TV Music

The Avengers • Doctor Who XI • Downton Abbey • Game of Thrones • Guardians of the Galaxy • Hawaii Five-O • Married Life • Rey's Theme (from *Star Wars: The Force Awakens*) • The X-Files • and more.

____	00261807	Flute	$12.99
____	00261808	Clarinet	$12.99
____	00261809	Alto Sax	$12.99
____	00261810	Tenor Sax	$12.99
____	00261811	Trumpet	$12.99
____	00261812	Horn	$12.99
____	00261813	Trombone	$12.99
____	00261814	Violin	$12.99
____	00261815	Viola	$12.99
____	00261816	Cello	$12.99

12 Pop Hits

Believer • Can't Stop the Feeling • Despacito • It Ain't Me • Look What You Made Me Do • Million Reasons • Perfect • Send My Love (To Your New Lover) • Shape of You • Slow Hands • Too Good at Goodbyes • What About Us.

____	00261790	Flute	$12.99
____	00261791	Clarinet	$12.99
____	00261792	Alto Sax	$12.99
____	00261793	Tenor Sax	$12.99
____	00261794	Trumpet	$12.99
____	00261795	Horn	$12.99
____	00261796	Trombone	$12.99
____	00261797	Violin	$12.99
____	00261798	Viola	$12.99
____	00261799	Cello	$12.99

Songs from Frozen, Tangled and Enchanted

Do You Want to Build a Snowman? • For the First Time in Forever • Happy Working Song • I See the Light • In Summer • Let It Go • Mother Knows Best • That's How You Know • True Love's First Kiss • When Will My Life Begin • and more.

____	00126921	Flute	$14.99
____	00126922	Clarinet	$14.99
____	00126923	Alto Sax	$14.99
____	00126924	Tenor Sax	$14.99
____	00126925	Trumpet	$14.99
____	00126926	Horn	$14.99
____	00126927	Trombone	$14.99
____	00126928	Violin	$14.99
____	00126929	Viola	$14.99
____	00126930	Cello	$14.99

Top Hits

Adventure of a Lifetime • Budapest • Die a Happy Man • Ex's & Oh's • Fight Song • Hello • Let It Go • Love Yourself • One Call Away • Pillowtalk • Stitches • Writing's on the Wall.

____	00171073	Flute	$12.99
____	00171074	Clarinet	$12.99
____	00171075	Alto Sax	$12.99
____	00171106	Tenor Sax	$12.99
____	00171107	Trumpet	$12.99
____	00171108	Horn	$12.99
____	00171109	Trombone	$12.99
____	00171110	Violin	$12.99
____	00171111	Viola	$12.99
____	00171112	Cello	$12.99

Wicked

As Long As You're Mine • Dancing Through Life • Defying Gravity • For Good • I'm Not That Girl • Popular • The Wizard and I • and more.

____	00842236	Flute	$12.99
____	00842237	Clarinet	$12.99
____	00842238	Alto Saxophone	$12.99
____	00842239	Tenor Saxophone	$11.95
____	00842240	Trumpet	$12.99
____	00842241	Horn	$12.99
____	00842242	Trombone	$12.99
____	00842243	Violin	$12.99
____	00842244	Viola	$12.99
____	00842245	Cello	$12.99

HAL•LEONARD®

101 SONGS

BIG COLLECTIONS OF FAVORITE SONGS ARRANGED FOR SOLO INSTRUMENTALISTS.

101 BROADWAY SONGS

00154199	Flute	$14.99
00154200	Clarinet	$14.99
00154201	Alto Sax	$14.99
00154202	Tenor Sax	$14.99
00154203	Trumpet	$14.99
00154204	Horn	$14.99
00154205	Trombone	$14.99
00154206	Violin	$14.99
00154207	Viola	$14.99
00154208	Cello	$14.99

101 HIT SONGS

00194561	Flute	$16.99
00197182	Clarinet	$16.99
00197183	Alto Sax	$16.99
00197184	Tenor Sax	$16.99
00197185	Trumpet	$16.99
00197186	Horn	$16.99
00197187	Trombone	$16.99
00197188	Violin	$16.99
00197189	Viola	$16.99
00197190	Cello	$16.99

101 CHRISTMAS SONGS

00278637	Flute	$14.99
00278638	Clarinet	$14.99
00278639	Alto Sax	$14.99
00278640	Tenor Sax	$14.99
00278641	Trumpet	$14.99
00278642	Horn	$14.99
00278643	Trombone	$14.99
00278644	Violin	$14.99
00278645	Viola	$14.99
00278646	Cello	$14.99

101 JAZZ SONGS

00146363	Flute	$14.99
00146364	Clarinet	$14.99
00146366	Alto Sax	$14.99
00146367	Tenor Sax	$14.99
00146368	Trumpet	$14.99
00146369	Horn	$14.99
00146370	Trombone	$14.99
00146371	Violin	$14.99
00146372	Viola	$14.99
00146373	Cello	$14.99

101 CLASSICAL THEMES

00155315	Flute	$14.99
00155317	Clarinet	$14.99
00155318	Alto Sax	$14.99
00155319	Tenor Sax	$14.99
00155320	Trumpet	$14.99
00155321	Horn	$14.99
00155322	Trombone	$14.99
00155323	Violin	$14.99
00155324	Viola	$14.99
00155325	Cello	$14.99

101 MOVIE HITS

00158087	Flute	$14.99
00158088	Clarinet	$14.99
00158089	Alto Sax	$14.99
00158090	Tenor Sax	$14.99
00158091	Trumpet	$14.99
00158092	Horn	$14.99
00158093	Trombone	$14.99
00158094	Violin	$14.99
00158095	Viola	$14.99
00158096	Cello	$14.99

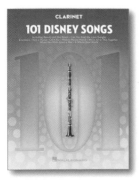

101 DISNEY SONGS

00244104	Flute	$16.99
00244106	Clarinet	$16.99
00244107	Alto Sax	$16.99
00244108	Tenor Sax	$16.99
00244109	Trumpet	$16.99
00244112	Horn	$16.99
00244120	Trombone	$16.99
00244121	Violin	$16.99
00244125	Viola	$16.99
00244126	Cello	$16.99

101 POPULAR SONGS

00224722	Flute	$16.99
00224723	Clarinet	$16.99
00224724	Alto Sax	$16.99
00224725	Tenor Sax	$16.99
00224726	Trumpet	$16.99
00224727	Horn	$16.99
00224728	Trombone	$16.99
00224729	Violin	$16.99
00224730	Viola	$16.99
00224731	Cello	$16.99

HAL•LEONARD®

www.halleonard.com

Prices, contents and availability subject to change without notice.